F
BAGUETTE
TO
BONJOUR

A FUN JOURNEY TO SPEAKING FRENCH

Brisa A.P.

FROM BAGUETTE TO BONJOUR

© Copyright 2023 by Brisa A. P.

CONTENTS

Preface

Welcome to From Baguette to Bonjour: A Fun Journey to Speaking French!

Learning a new language can seem daunting at first but fear not! With this guide, you'll be well on your way to understanding and speaking French in no time.

Whether you're traveling to France, have French-speaking friends, or just want to expand your linguistic abilities, this book is the perfect resource for you. The lessons are designed to take you step by step through the basics of French grammar and vocabulary, so even if you have no prior experience with the language, you'll be able to follow along.

But this isn't just any old dry language textbook. We've spiced up the learning process with fun and engaging exercises, as well as useful tips and cultural insights to help you really immerse yourself in the language. Our goal is not just to teach you French, but to help you love it!

So whether you're studying alone or with a group, take your time and enjoy the learning process. And don't forget to practice your skills in real-world situations. Bonne chance!

Introduction

Welcome to *From Baguette to Bonjour: A Fun Journey to Speaking French,* , an ebook designed to help English speakers learn the basics of the French language. Whether you're planning a trip to France, or simply want to expand your language skills, this audiobook is the perfect starting point.

In this ebook, you will find a comprehensive guide to French pronunciation, grammar, and vocabulary, presented in an easy-to-follow format. Each lesson is carefully structured to build upon the previous lesson, helping you to gradually master the language.

From common French phrases and greetings to essential grammar rules and verb conjugation, *From Baguette to Bonjour* will provide you with a solid introduction to the language. We will guide you through each lesson, providing practical tips and helpful examples along the way.

Learning a new language can be challenging, but it can also be incredibly rewarding. With *From Baguette to Bonjour,* you will be on your way to speaking French with confidence. So, let's get started!

Chapter 1

French Alphabet and Pronunciation

In this chapter, we will cover the French alphabet and pronunciation. You will be introduced to some of the unique sounds and accents of the French language through the correct pronunciation of each letter. With this foundation in pronunciation, you'll be well on your way to mastering the sounds of French with confidence.

The French Alphabet

Even though French and English use the same alphabet, the pronunciation of the letters in French differs slightly. This difference means that when you need to spell out words in French, such as your name at a hotel, it is important to ensure that the person listening can understand you clearly.

Letter	Pronunciation
A	ah
B	bay
C	say
D	day
E	euh
F	eff
G	zhay
H	ash
I	ee
J	jee
K	kah
L	ell
M	emm
N	enn
O	oh
P	pay
Q	koo
R	air
S	ess
T	tay
U	ooh
V	vay

W	doobluh-vay
X	eex
Y	ee-grek
Z	zed

When pronouncing letters in French, there are a few key points to keep in mind:

- The letter "e" in French sounds similar to the beginning of the English word "earl."

- The letter "g" is pronounced with a soft "j" sound, similar to the "j" in "Asia."

- The letter "j" also uses a soft "j" sound, but with an "ee" sound at the end.

- When "n" appears at the end of words, it is pronounced softly with a nasal quality.

- The French "q" is pronounced with a "ooh" sound, similar to English, but without the "y" sound.

- When two "l"s appear together, they create a "yeh" sound, different from the pronunciation of a single "l."

- Finally, the French "r" is made at the back of the throat and has a more guttural quality compared to the English "r."

The French Sounds

The majority of consonants in French are pronounced the same way as in English. However, the two languages diverge in the pronunciation of vowels. Because it is difficult to represent the true sound of spoken French through text, you should listen to actual French being spoken – whether through music, film, or television. Listening to native or bilingual speakers will help you to appreciate the nuances in sound. Nonetheless, here is a list of sounds commonly used in the French language, along with words to practice pronouncing aloud:

- "on" sounds similar to "oh" in English with a soft "n" at the end, found in words like "maison" (meh-zohn, meaning "house") and "garçon" (gar-sohn, meaning "boy").

- "ou" is pronounced like "ooh" and appears in words like "tout" (tooh, meaning "all").

- "oi" makes a "wha" sound, similar to the beginning of the English word "waddle," as heard in French words like "soir" (swahr, meaning "evening").

- "oin" sounds like the start of "when" in English, with a soft "n" sound that is barely audible. "Coin" (kwheh, meaning "corner") and "moins" (mwheh, meaning "less") are examples.

- "ai" sounds like "ehh" and appears in many words, including "maison" and "vrai" (vreh, meaning "true").

- "en" sounds similar to "on" in English, but with a much softer "n" sound. This sound is found in words such as "encore" (ahnk-ohr, meaning "again") and "parent" (pahr-ahn, meaning "parent").

- "an" is pronounced the same way as "en."

- "eu" requires holding your mouth like you're going to make an "eee" sound but saying "oooh" instead, similar to the start of the English word "earl." "Heure" (ehhr, meaning "hour") is an example.

- "in" is pronounced like the start of the English word "enter" but with a much softer "n" sound. Examples include "magasin" (may-guh-zehn, meaning "store") and "pain" (pehn, meaning "bread").

- "er" sounds like "ayy" and is commonly found at the end of verbs such as "parler" (parl-ay, meaning "to speak") and "entrer" (ahn-tray, meaning "to enter").

Practicing French Sounds:

Sound	French Examples	English Translation
"on"	maison, garçon, chanson	house, boy, song
"ou"	tout, ouest, cou	all, west, neck
"oi"	soir, bois, voilà	evening, wood, there
"oin"	coin, moins, loin	corner, less, far
"ai"	maison, vrai, mais	house, true, but
"en"	encore, parent, lent	still, relative, slow
"an"	temps, avant, sang	time, before, blood
"eu"	heure, jeune, deux	hour, young, two
"in"	magasin, pain, vin	shop, bread, wine
"er"	parler, entrer, manger	to speak, to enter, to eat

Pronouncing "H" and the Rolled "R"

In French, the letter "h" is typically silent at the beginning of words, and the pronunciation is as if the "h" were absent. This phenomenon is known as "h muet" or a silent letter in French. However, there are a few exceptions where the "h" is pronounced, the "h aspiré." These nuances as well as the French language's tendency to run words together can make it challenging for beginners to understand spoken French. This situation is further complicated by the shortening of words, formation of contractions, and the pushing together of syllables, making multiple words sound like a single long word.

Sound	Examples with "h muet"	Examples with "h aspiré"
H	homme (man)	haricot (bean)
	histoire (story)	hôpital (hospital)
	hôtel (hotel)	hiver (winter)
	hier (yesterday)	
	hasard (chance)	
	homme (man)	

The French language is often characterized by the distinct rolling "r" sound, and you too can learn how to produce it with some practice. To begin, try producing a "k" sound and hold it. Then, slightly constrict your throat, exhale slowly, and start to say the word "raw." Don't be discouraged if it initially comes out sounding more like "graw." With persistence and repetition, you can perfect the technique and achieve the same sound as iconic French singer Edith Piaf.

Sound	Example 1	Example 2	Example 3
Rolled "r"	voiture (car)	croissant (croissant)	parcours (course)
	brûler (to burn)	arbre (tree)	terre (earth)
	quatre (four)	partir (to leave)	rouge (red)

Do not hesitate to speak French as French speakers tend to be very tolerant and patient when conversing with those who are new to the language. Generally, native French speakers are delighted when someone tries to communicate in their language, and they are typically keen to assist in your comprehension. French will likely be accommodating of your beginner's level French skills, so do not be afraid to express yourself.

Chapter 2

Get Prepared to Speak French Like a Native

This section presents a variety of everyday expressions that may not always have a direct translation though they are widely used and understood by French speakers. Additionally, the chapter offers insights into common greetings and fundamental numerical concepts.

Practical and Informal Phrases for Everyday Communication

Expression	Meaning	Literal Translation	Type
Comment allez-vous?	How are you?	How are you going?	Idiomatic
Comment vous appelez-vous?	What is your name?	How do you call yourself?	Idiomatic
Je ne parle pas français.	I don't speak French.	N/A	Idiomatic

Parlez-vous anglais?	Do you speak English?	Speak you English?	Idiomatic
C'est la vie.	That's life.	That is the life.	Idiomatic
J'ai faim.	I'm hungry.	I have hunger.	Idiomatic
Ça ne fait rien.	It doesn't matter.	That doesn't make anything.	Idiomatic
Qu'est-ce que c'est?	What is it?	What is that it?	Idiomatic
Bon appétit.	Enjoy your meal.	Good appetite.	Colloquial
À tes souhaits.	Bless you.	To your wishes.	Colloquial
À la prochaine.	See you next time.	Until the next time.	Colloquial

Note: "Idiomatic" expressions are unique to the language and cannot be translated literally, while "colloquial" expressions are widely recognized in the language and are acceptable to use in everyday speech, despite bending the rules of grammar.

Salutation and Greetings

The following chart includes vocabulary words and phrases that can be used as basic greetings or responses when communicating with friends and family. These expressions are simple enough to easily remember.

French Greeting	Pronunciation	English Translation	Usage
Salut	sah-LOO	Hi/Hello	Informal greeting, used with friends and family

Bonjour	bohn-ZHOOR	Good morning/afternoon	Standard greeting used throughout the day
Bonsoir	bohn-SWAHR	Good evening	Standard greeting used in the evening
Coucou	koo-KOO	Hey/Hi	Informal greeting, used with close friends and family
Bienvenue	byan-venn-oo	Welcome	Used to greet someone who has arrived
Au revoir	oh ruh-VWAHR	Goodbye	Standard farewell used throughout the day
Bonne journée	bawn zhoor-nay	Have a good day	Used to wish someone a good day
Bonne soirée	bawn swah-ray	Have a good evening	Used to wish someone a good evening

Remembering the correct pronunciations for these expressions will go a long way in making you sound natural when speaking French.

Learn Numbers and Dates

French uses the same numerical symbols as English, which are known as chiffres arabes. However, the pronunciation of numbers is different. You'll need to memorize the names of the numbers and how larger numbers are constructed. As with English, there are two kinds of numbers: cardinal and ordinal numbers. Cardinal numbers indicate an amount of something whereas ordinal numbers represent placement in a series.

Cardinal Numbers

Let's start with cardinal numbers!

Numbers ranging from zero to nineteen are relatively simple.

English	French	Pronunciation
One	un	ahn
Two	deux	deuh
three	trois	twa
Four	quatre	katr
Five	cinq	sank
Six	six	sees
seven	sept	set
eight	huit	hweet
nine	neuf	nuhf
ten	dix	dees
eleven	onze	ohnz
twelve	douze	dooz
thirteen	treize	trehz

English	French	Pronunciation
fourteen	quatorze	kah-torz
fifteen	quinze	cans
sixteen	seize	sez
seventeen	dix-sept	dees-set
eighteen	dix-huit	dees-hweet
nineteen	dix-neuf	dees-nuhf

The pattern for naming numbers from twenty to sixty-nine in French is consistent and similar to English, where a group of tens, such as "twenty," is followed by a unit, such as "one" to create "twenty-one." These numbers are written with a hyphen, except for "et un," which consists of two words and means "and one."

English	French	Pronunciation
twenty	vingt	vahn
twenty-one	vingt et un	vahn tay uhN
twenty-two	vingt-deux	vahn duh
twenty-three	vingt-trois	vahn twa
twenty-four	vingt-quatre	vahn katr
twenty-five	vingt-cinq	vahn sank
twenty-six	vingt-six	vahn sees

twenty-seven	vingt-sept	vahn set
twenty-eight	vingt-huit	vahn hweet
twenty-nine	vingt-neuf	vahn nuhf

To create numbers ranging from thirty to sixty-nine, you can simply append the corresponding digit after the word for the tens place.

English	French	Pronunciation
thirty	trente	trahnt
thirty-one	trente et un	trahnt ay uhn
thirty-two	trente-deux	trahnt deuh
thirty-three	trente-trois	trahnt twa
thirty-four	trente-quatre	trahnt katr
thirty-five	trente-cinq	trahnt sank
thirty-six	trente-six	trahnt sees
thirty-seven	trente-sept	trahnt set
thirty-eight	trente-huit	trahnt hweet
thirty-nine	trente-neuf	trahnt nuhf
forty	quarante	karant
forty-one	quarante et un	karant ay uhn

forty-two	quarante-deux	karant deuh
forty-three	quarante-trois	karant twa
forty-four	quarante-quatre	karant katr
forty-five	quarante-cinq	karant sank
forty-six	quarante-six	karant sees
forty-seven	quarante-sept	karant set
forty-eight	quarante-huit	karant hweet
forty-nine	quarante-neuf	karant nuhf
fifty	cinquante	sankahnt
fifty-one	cinquante et un	sankahnt ay uhn
fifty-two	cinquante-deux	sankahnt deuh
fifty-three	cinquante-trois	sankahnt twa
fifty-four	cinquante-quatre	sankahnt katr
fifty-five	cinquante-cinq	sankahnt sank
fifty-six	cinquante-six	sankahnt sees
fifty-seven	cinquante-sept	sankahnt set
fifty-eight	cinquante-huit	sankahnt hweet
fifty-nine	cinquante-neuf	sankahnt nuhf
sixty	soixante	swasant

English	French	Pronunciation
sixty-one	soixante et un	swasant ay uhn
sixty-two	soixante-deux	swasant deuh
sixty-three	soixante-trois	swasant twa
sixty-four	soixante-quatre	swasant katr
sixty-five	soixante-cinq	swasant sank
sixty-six	soixante-six	swasant sees
sixty-seven	soixante-sept	swasant set
sixty-eight	soixante-huit	swasant hweet
sixty-nine	soixante-neuf	swasant nuhf

In French, the words for "seventy" and "eighty" are formed by combining the words for "sixty" and "ten" and "four twenties", respectively. The numbers from eleven to nineteen are used to designate numbers up to seventy-nine, and ninety is formed by combining "four twenties" and "ten". In written French, eighty-one is written as "four twenties one" without the traditional conjunction of "and."

English	French	Pronunciation
seventy	soixante-dix	swa-sont-dees
seventy-one	soixante-et-onze	swa-sont-ay-ohnz
seventy-two	soixante-douze	swa-sont-dooz

seventy-three	soixante-treize	swa-sont-trehz
seventy-four	soixante-quatorze	swa-sont-kah-torz
seventy-five	soixante-quinze	swa-sont-cans
seventy-six	soixante-seize	swa-sont-sez
seventy-seven	soixante-dix-sept	swa-sont-dees-set
seventy-eight	soixante-dix-huit	swa-sont-dees-hweet
seventy-nine	soixante-dix-neuf	swa-sont-dees-nuhf
eighty	quatre-vingt	catruh-van
eighty-one	quatre-vingt-un	catruh-van-ahn
eighty-two	quatre-vingt-deux	catruh-van-deuh
eighty-three	quatre-vingt-trois	catruh-van-twa
eighty-four	quatre-vingt-quatre	catruh-van-katr
eighty-five	quatre-vingt-cinq	catruh-van-sank
eighty-six	quatre-vingt-six	catruh-van-sees
eighty-seven	quatre-vingt-sept	catruh-van-set
eighty-eight	quatre-vingt-huit	catruh-van-hweet
eighty-nine	quatre-vingt-neuf	catruh-van-nuhf
ninety	quatre-vingt-dix	catruh-van-dees
ninety-one	quatre-vingt-onze	catruh-van-ohnz

ninety-two	quatre-vingt-douze	catruh-van-dooz
ninety-three	quatre-vingt-treize	catruh-van-trehz
ninety-four	quatre-vingt-quatorze	catruh-van-kah-torz
ninety-five	quatre-vingt-quinze	catruh-van-cans
ninety-six	quatre-vingt-seize	catruh-van-sez
ninety-seven	quatre-vingt-dix-sept	catruh-van-dees-set
ninety-eight	quatre-vingt-dix-huit	catruh-van-dees-hweet
ninety-nine	quatre-vingt-dix-neuf	catruh-van-dees-nuhf

In French, the term for 100 is "cent." It followed by the appropriate number to indicate numbers between 101 and 199.

Number	French	Pronunciation
100	cent	sahn
101	cent un	sahn uhn
102	cent deux	sahn deuh
103	cent trois	sahn twa
104	cent quatre	sahn katr
105	cent cinq	sahn sank

106	cent six	sahn sees
107	cent sept	sahn set
108	cent huit	sahn hweet
109	cent neuf	sahn nuhf
110	cent dix	sahn dees
111	cent onze	sahn ohnz
112	cent douze	sahn dooz
113	cent treize	sahn trehz
114	cent quatorze	sahn kah-torz
115	cent quinze	sahn cans
116	cent seize	sahn sez
117	cent dix-sept	sahn dees-set
118	cent dix-huit	sahn dees-hweet
119	cent dix-neuf	sahn dees-nuhf
120	cent vingt	sahn vahn

In French, to express numbers greater than one hundred, you simply use the specific number to indicate how many hundreds followed by "cent." This process is similar to the English language, in which the only difference between "one hundred" and "two hundred" is the number at the beginning. However, in French, when the number is a multiple of one hundred, the word "cent" is pluralized with an "s" at the end, even though it is not pronounced. This is an important distinction to keep in mind when writing in French.

Number	French	Pronunciation
200	deux cents	duh sahn
300	trois cents	twa sahn
400	quatre cents	katr sahn
500	cinq cents	sank sahn
600	six cents	sees sahn
700	sept cents	set sahn
800	huit cents	hweet sahn
900	neuf cents	nuhf sahn
999	neuf cent quatre-vingt-dix-neuf	nuhf sahn katr-van-neuf-dees-nuhf

The word for "one thousand" or "mille" in French follows the same pattern as "one hundred." However, unlike "one hundred," mille does not take the plural "s" when spelling out numbers.

Number	French	Pronunciation
1,000	Mille	meel
10,000	dix mille	dees meel
50,000	cinquante mille	sankont meel
100,000	cent mille	sahn meel
500,000	cinq cent mille	sank sahn meel
1,000,000	un million	ahn mee-lyohn
2,000,000	deux millions	duh mee-lyohn

When referring to a year, the date follows this pattern of spelling as well. In spoken French, talking about years can sometimes be a mouthful. For example:

- 1939: mille neuf cent trente-neuf (mee-yh noof sahn trahnt nuhf)

- 1956: mille neuf cent cinquante-six (mee-yh noof sahn sank-ahn-tee-sees)

- 1971: mille neuf cent soixante-et-onze (mee-yh noof sahn swah-zahnt ay ohnz)

Thankfully, recent years are much simpler. Deux mille is easier to remember and to pronounce.

Ordinal Numbers

As with English, French has its own way to say "first," "second," "third," and so on…

"First" or premier in French has a different ending, depending on whether the noun that modifies is masculine or feminine. It may also be pluralized as necessary, though the "s" remains silent.

Gender	Singular	Plural	Pronunciation
Masculine	Premier	premiers	pruh-mee-yay
Feminine	Première	premières	pruh-mee-aihr

The remaining ordinal numbers do not vary in gender agreement, though they require an "s" to match a plural noun.

Number	French	Pronunciation
2nd	deuxième	douz-yehm
3rd	troisième	twa-zee-yehm
4th	quatrième	ka-tree-yehm
5th	cinquième	sank-yehm
6th	sixième	sees-yehm
7th	septième	set-yehm
8th	huitième	hweet-yehm
9th	neuvième	nuh-vee-yehm
10th	dixième	dee-z-yehm

To form ordinal numbers in French, you do not need to memorize them all; you can learn to create them on your own. The cardinal number is used to form ordinal numbers, similarly to the way English creates ordinal numbers by adding "th" to the end of the cardinal number, such as "fourth" from "four," "fifth" from "five," "sixth" from "six," and so on.

Now, let see how to use the abbreviations of ordinal numbers:

English	French	Pronunciation	Abbreviation
first	premier (m)	pruh-mee-yay	1er
first	première (f)	pruh-mee-aihr	1re
second	deuxième	doo-zee-ehm	2e
third	troisième	twah-zee-ehm	3e
fourth	quatrième	kah-tree-ehm	4e
fifth	cinquième	sank-yem	5e
sixth	sixième	sees-yem	6e
seventh	septième	set-yem	7e
eighth	huitième	hweet-yem	8e
ninth	neuvième	nuh-vee-yem	9e
tenth	dixième	dee-zee-yem	10e

When you encounter these abbreviations in various forms of written French, such as in newspapers, books, signs, and magazines, you should recognize that they represent ordinal numbers.

The Dates in French

Learning French involves memorizing basic words such as the days of the week and months of the year. Practicing the following lists out loud can help you memorize them more easily. When recited consecutively, they have a catchy rhythm that can help you memorize them quickly.

The Days of the Week

English	French	Pronunciation
Monday	lundi	loon-dee
Tuesday	mardi	mar-dee
Wednesday	mercredi	mair-cruh-dee
Thursday	jeudi	zhuh-dee
Friday	vendredi	vahn-druh-dee
Saturday	samedi	sahm-dee
Sunday	dimanche	dee-mahnsh

The Months

English	French	Pronunciation
January	janvier	zhan-vee-ay
February	février	feh-vree-ay

March	mars	mahr
April	avril	ah-vreel
May	mai	may
June	juin	zhwan
July	juillet	zhwee-yay
August	août	ah-oot
September	septembre	sep-tahm-bruh
October	octobre	ok-toh-bruh
November	novembre	noh-vahm-bruh
December	décembre	deh-sahm-bruh

When writing in French, it is not necessary to capitalize the days of the week or months of the year, unless they are used at the start of a sentence.

Chapter 3

Learn some Basic Vocabulary in French

This chapter aims to assist you in acquiring a fundamental vocabulary that will contribute to your conversations with native French speakers. It begins with basic conjunctions (i.e., words like "and," "or," and "but" in English) and progresses through a collection of fundamental terms and expressions.

Mastering French Conjunctions

Conjunctions serve the purpose of connecting different parts of a sentence. In the English language, words like "and," "or," and "but" are the most common conjunctions. Similarly, you can use the following French conjunctions in the same manner as their English counterparts:

French	Pronunciation	English Translation
et	ay	and
ou	oo	or
mais	may	but
car	kar	for, because
donc	donk	so, therefore
or	or	yet, however
ni	nee	neither, nor
que	kuh	only, that
lorsque	lor-sk	when
avant que	avahn kuh	before
après que	ap-ray kuh	after

Basic French Vocabulary for Everyday Conversation

This vocabulary list contains a selection of foundational conversational words and phrases that you can easily learn and remember. These words are frequently used in French conversations, so mastering them now will help you communicate more effectively.

French	Pronunciation	English
oui	wee	yes
non	noh	no
merci	mehr-see	thank you
s'il vous plaît, s'il te plaît	seel voo play, seel te play	please
excusez-moi, excuse-moi	ex-kew-zay mwah, ex-kewz mwah	excuse me
pardon	pahr-dohn	sorry, pardon me
au revoir	oh ruh-vwahr	goodbye
bonjour	bawn-zhoor	hello, good morning
bonsoir	bawn-swahr	good evening
salut	sah-lyoo	hi, bye

Now that you know some basic vocabulary, let's go a little bit further so you can speak in different situations.

Whether you are visiting France for a holiday or planning to stay there, you will need a minimum of vocabulary for everyday life, such as going to a restaurant, paying for tickets, fares, or other items, asking for directions… In short, for many situations.

Navigating Transportation in France

Let's begin by learning the terms for different types of transportation in French:

English	French	Pronunciation
car	la voiture	lah vwah-tuhr
bus	le bus	luh boos
train	le train	luh trahn
plane	l'avion	lah-vee-yohn
bike	le vélo	luh veh-loh
taxi	le taxi	luh tahk-see
subway	le métro	luh meh-troh
boat	le bateau	luh ba-toh
walk	la marche	lah mahrsh
run	la course	lah koors
ferry	le ferry	luh feh-ree
motorcycle	la moto	lah moh-toh

You may be more likely to come to France by plane, so let's learn some vocabulary that can be useful at the airport.

Useful vocabulary at the airport:

English	French	Pronunciation
airport	l'aéroport	lay-roh-por
airline	la compagnie aérienne	lah kohm-pah-nee ay-ree-enn
flight	le vol	luh vohl
ticket	le billet	luh bee-yay
boarding pass	la carte d'embarquement	lah kahrt dahn-barck-mohn
baggage	les bagages	lay bah-gazh
luggage	les valises	lay va-leez
carry-on luggage	le bagage à main	luh bah-gazh ah mahn
checked luggage	le bagage enregistré	luh bah-gazh ahn-rehzhee-stray
customs	la douane	lah doo-ahn
passport	le passeport	luh pahs-por
security check	le contrôle de sécurité	luh kohn-trohl duh say-cure-ee-tay
gate	la porte d'embarquement	lah port dahn-barck-mohn
delay	le retard	luh ruh-tard
cancellation	l'annulation	lah-noon-syoh
connecting flight	la correspondance	lah kohr-respond-ahns

Once you have arrived in France, especially if you come to Paris, you will probably have to take the train, the bus, or the subway. Let's learn some more vocabulary!

Useful vocabulary to take the bus, the subway, or the train:

English	French	Pronunciation
bus	le bus/l'autobus	luh boos/loh-toh-boos
subway/underground	le metro	luh may-troh
train	le train	luh trahn
station	la gare	lah gahr
ticket	le billet	luh bee-yay
one way ticket	l'aller simple	lah-lay sahmpl
round trip ticket	l'aller-retour	lah-lay ruh-toor
schedule	l'horaire	loh-rair
platform	le quai	luh kai
arrival	l'arrivée	lah-ree-vay
departure	le départ	luh day-par
delay	le retard	luh ruh-tard
cancelled	annulé	ahn-yoo-lay
connection	la correspondance	lah kohr-spoh-dahns

Staying at Hotels in France

English	French	Pronunciation
hotel	l'hôtel	lo-tell
reception	la réception	lah ray-sep-see-yohn
room	la chambre	lah shahm-bruh
reservation	la réservation	lah ray-zair-vay-syon
key	la clé	lah clay
check-in	l'arrivée / l'enregistrement	lar-ree-vay / lah-nair-zhe-straw-mawn
check-out	le départ	luh day-par
breakfast	le petit déjeuner	luh puh-tee day-zhuh-nay
lunch	le déjeuner	luh day-zhuh-nay
dinner	le dîner	luh dee-nay
menu	le menu	luh muh-new
wi-fi	le wi-fi	luh wee-fee
bill	l'addition	lah-dee-see-yohn
credit card	la carte de crédit	lah kart duh kray-dee
cash	l'argent liquide	lahr-zhahn lee-keed
reservation confirmation	la confirmation de réservation	lah kawn-fer-mah-see-yohn duh ray-zair-vay-syon

If you come to France on a trip, you may stay at an hotel. This offers us the opportunity to learn even more vocabulary... Hooray!

Activities to do in France

Whether you visit Paris, other cities, or the countryside, you will probably want to do participate in different activities. Let's discover different activities in French.

English	French	Pronunciation
visit museums	visiter des musées	vee-ze-tay day moo-zay
explore cities	explorer des villes	ex-plo-ray day veels
try French cuisine	essayer la cuisine française	ess-aye-ay la kwee-zeen frahn-sayz
drink wine	boire du vin	bwahr doo van
visit landmarks	visiter des sites touristiques	vee-ze-tay day seet too-ree-stik
attend festivals	assister à des festivals	ah-see-stay ah day fes-teevahl
go to the beach	aller à la plage	ah-lay ah lah plahzh
ski in the mountains	skier dans les montagnes	skeer dan lay mohn-tahn
hike in nature	faire de la randonnée	fair duh lah ran-doh-nay
shop in markets	faire du shopping dans les marchés	fair duh shoppang dan lay mar-shay

Unfortunately, we can't give you an exhaustive list of activities that you could do in France. Perhaps we'll make an ebook of them (LOL).

Money Matters in France

If there's one thing you're going to need in France, it's money. France is indeed not necessarily the most affordable country, especially if you are visiting the big cities or tourist places.

English	French	Pronunciation
money	l'argent	lar-zhahn
cash	liquide	lee-keed
credit card	carte de crédit	kart duh kray-dee
ATM	distributeur automatique	dee-stree-byoo-teur oh-toh-ma-teek
exchange	change	shahnj
bank	banque	bahnk
account	compte	kohnt
deposit	dépôt	day-poh
withdrawal	retrait	ruh-tray
bill	facture	fak-tur
tip	pourboire	poor-bwar
price	prix	pree
tax	taxe	tahks
receipt	ticket	tee-kay

Ordering Food in French Restaurants

You cannot go to France without visiting traditional restaurants to try French gastronomy. Let's discover useful vocabulary for visiting restaurants.

English	French	Pronunciation
menu	menu	meh-noo
water	eau	oh
bread	pain	pahn
butter	beurre	buhr
appetizer	entrée	ahn-tray
main dish	plat principal	plah prahn-see-pahl
dessert	dessert	deh-sehr
bill	addition/note	ah-dee-see-yon/note
tip	pourboire	poor-bwahr
waiter	serveur	sehr-veur
waitress	serveuse	sehr-veuhz
table	table	tah-bluh
reservation	réservation	reh-zer-vah-see-yon
fork	fourchette	foohr-shet
knife	couteau	koo-toh
spoon	cuillère	kwee-yair
plate	assiette	ah-syet
glass	verre	vehr
wine	vin	vahn
beer	bière	byehr

Ordering Drinks in French Cafés and Bars

You may decide to forgo restaurants to enjoy a coffee or refresh yourself in a bar. Let's discover useful vocabulary for a café or bar.

English	French	Pronunciation
coffee	café	kah-fay
tea	tThé	tay
espresso	espresso	es-press-oh
cappuccino	cappuccino	kah-poo-chee-noh
latte	café au lait	kah-fay oh lay
hot chocolate	chocolat chaud	sho-koh-lah shoh
croissant	croissant	kwah-sahn
pastry	pâtisserie	pah-tees-ree
sandwich	sandwich	sahn-dee-sh
beer	bière	byehr
wine	vin	vahn
cocktail	cocktail	kohk-teyl
whiskey	whisky	wees-kee
vodka	vodka	voh-dkah
ice	glace	glahs
straw	paille	pahy
napkin	serviette	sehr-vyeh-tuh
tip	pourboire	poor-bwahr
bill	addition/note	ah-dee-see-yon/note

waiter	serveur	sehr-veur
waitress	serveuse	sehr-veuhz
table	table	tah-bluh
reservation	réservation	reh-zer-vah-see-yon

Shopping in France: Vocabulary You Need to Know

Perhaps you would like to buy souvenirs to remember your trip. Besides, isn't Paris the capital of fashion and great gastronomy? How could you visit without shopping? Prepare your wallet and let's learn some vocabulary to go shopping.

English	French	Pronunciation
store	magasin	mah-gah-sahn
market	marché	mar-shay
supermarket	supermarché	soo-pehr-mahr-shay
shop	boutique	boo-teek
department store	grand magasin	grahnd mah-gah-sahn
clothing	vêtements	vet-mahn
shoes	chaussures	shoosoor
accessories	accessoires	ahk-seh-swahr
groceries	épicerie	ay-pee-suh-ree
fruit	fruits	frwee
vegetables	légumes	lay-guhm

bakery	boulangerie	boo-lahn-juh-ree
butcher's shop	boucherie	boo-shuh-ree
fishmonger's shop	poissonnerie	pwah-sohn-uh-ree
cashier	caissier/caissière	kah-see-yay/kah-see-air
receipt	ticket	tee-kay
credit card	carte de crédit	kart duh kray-dee
cash	argent liquide	ahr-zhahn lee-keed
discount	réduction	ray-dook-see-yon
sale	solde	sol-duh
price	prix	pree

Chapter 4

French Conjugation

This is often the most dreaded part of learning any language. However, if you want to learn to speak French, you will have no choice but to learn conjugation. But don't worry, we will go easy…

Present Time: "To Be" and "To Have" Present Time – Verbs in French in Present Time

Before jumping right into the present conjugation in French, we are going to learn the verbs "to be" and "to have", which are certainly the most important verbs, though not necessarily the simplest...

"To be" and "to have" in French – Present tense:

English (to be)	French (être)	English (to have)	French (avoir)
I am	je suis	I have	j'ai
You are	tu es	You have	tu as

He/She/It is	il/elle est	He/She/It has	il/elle a
We are	nous sommes	We have	nous avons
You are	vous êtes	You have	vous avez
They are	ils/elles sont	They have	ils/elles ont

Before going further into the conjugation of the present tense, let's learn the three groups of verbs in French: verbs ending in "-er," "-ir," and "-re." You will notice that these verbs take a certain pattern of endings in conjugation.

Verbs in French ending by "-er":

English	French
to love	aimer
to speak	parler
to eat	manger
to work	travailler
to walk	marcher
to play	jouer
to listen	écouter
to study	étudier
to sing	chanter
to swim	nager
to watch	regarder

to cook	cuisiner
to travel	voyager
to enter	entrer
to arrive	arriver
to buy	acheter
to sell	vendre
to call	appeler

Verbs in French ending by "-er" – Present Conjugation:

Pronoun	-er verb endings
je	-e
tu	-es
il/elle	-e
nous	-ons
vous	-ez
ils/elles	-ent

English	French Infinitive	Je (I)	Tu (singular you)	Il/Elle/On (he/she/one)	Nous (we)	Vous (plural you)	Ils/Elles (they)
to love	aimer	j'aime	tu aimes	il/elle/on aime	nous aimons	vous aimez	ils/elles aiment
to speak	parler	je parle	tu parles	il/elle/on parle	nous parlons	vous parlez	ils/elles parlent
to eat	manger	je mange	tu manges	il/elle/on mange	nous mangeons	vous mangez	ils/elles mangent
to work	travailler	je travaille	tu travailles	il/elle/on travaille	nous travaillons	vous travaillez	ils/elles travaillent
to walk	marcher	je marche	tu marches	il/elle/on marche	nous marchons	vous marchez	ils/elles marchent
to play	jouer	je joue	tu joues	il/elle/on joue	nous jouons	vous jouez	ils/elles jouent
to listen	écouter	j'écoute	tu écoutes	il/elle/on écoute	nous écoutons	vous écoutez	ils/elles écoutent
to study	étudier	j'étudie	tu étudies	il/elle/on étudie	nous étudions	vous étudiez	ils/elles étudient
to sing	chanter	je chante	tu chantes	il/elle/on chante	nous chantons	vous chantez	ils/elles chantent
to swim	nager	je nage	tu nages	il/elle/on nage	nous nageons	vous nagez	ils/elles nagent
to watch	regarder	je regarde	tu regardes	il/elle/on regarde	nous regardons	vous regardez	ils/elles regardent

to cook	cuisiner	je cuisine	tu cuisines	il/elle/on cuisine	nous cuisinons	vous cuisinez	ils/elles cuisinent

Verbs in French ending by "-ir" Present Conjugation:

English	French infinitive
to choose	choisir
to succeed	réussir
to finish	finir
to grow up	grandir
to invest	investir
to punish	punir
to reflect	réfléchir
to lose weight	maigrir
to obey	obéir
to build	bâtir
to accomplish	accomplir
to fill	remplir
to react	réagir
to think	réfléchir
to blush	rougir
to seize	saisir
to age	vieillir
to reunite	réunir
to convert	convertir

Verbs in French ending by "-ir" – French conjugation:

Pronoun	-ir verb endings
je	-is
tu	-is
il/elle	-it
nous	-issons
vous	-issez
ils/elles	-issent

English	French Infinitive	Je	Tu (singular you)	Il/Elle/On	Nous	Vous (plural you)	Ils/Elles
to choose	choisir	je choisis	tu choisis	il/elle/on choisit	nous choisissons	vous choisissez	ils/elles choisissent
to succeed	réussir	je réussis	tu réussis	il/elle/on réussit	nous réussissons	vous réussissez	ils/elles réussissent
to finish	finir	je finis	tu finis	il/elle/on finit	nous finissons	vous finissez	ils/elles finissent
to grow up	grandir	je grandis	tu grandis	il/elle/on grandit	nous grandissons	vous grandissez	ils/elles grandissent
to invest	investir	j'investis	tu investis	il/elle/on investit	nous investissons	vous investissez	ils/elles investissent
to punish	punir	je punis	tu punis	il/elle/on punit	nous punissons	vous punissez	ils/elles punissent

to reflect	réfléch ir	je réfléchi s	tu réfléchi s	il/elle/ on réfléchi t	nous réfléchisso ns	vous réfléchiss ez	ils/elles réfléchiss ent
to lose weight	maigrir	je maigris	tu maigris	il/elle/ on maigrit	nous maigrisson s	vous maigrisse z	ils/elles maigrisse nt
to obey	obéir	j'obéis	tu obéis	il/elle/ on obéit	nous obéissons	vous obéissez	ils/elles obéissent
to build	bâtir	je bâtis	tu bâtis	il/elle/ on bâtit	nous bâtissons	vous bâtissez	ils/elles bâtissent
to accompl ish	accom plir	j'accom plis	tu accom plis	il/elle/ on accomp lit	nous accomplis sons	vous accompli ssez	ils/elles accomplis sent
to fill	remplir	je remplis	tu remplis	il/elle/ on remplit	nous remplisso ns	vous remplisse z	ils/elles remplisse nt
to react	réagir	je réagis	tu réagis	il/elle/ on réagit	nous réagissons	vous réagissez	ils/elles réagissent
to think	réfléch ir	je réfléchi s	tu réfléchi s	il/elle/ on réfléchi t	nous réfléchisso ns	vous réfléchiss ez	ils/elles réfléchiss ent
to blush	rougir	je rougis	tu rougis	il/elle/ on rougit	nous rougissons	vous rougissez	ils/elles rougissent

Verbs in French ending by "-re" Present Conjugation:

English	French infinitive
to sell	vendre
to write	Écrire
to take	prendre
to learn	apprendre
to understand	comprendre
to put	mettre
to lose	perdre
to live	Vivre
to believe	croire
to hear	entendre
to repeat	répéter

Verbs in French ending by "-re" – French conjugation:

Pronoun	-re verb endings
je	-s
tu	-s
il/elle	-
nous	-ons
vous	-ez
ils/elles	-ent

English	French infinitive	Je (I)	Tu (singular you)	Il/Elle/On (he/she/one)	Nous (we)	Vous (plural you)	Ils/Elles (they)
to sell	vendre	je vends	tu vends	il/elle/on vend	nous vendons	vous vendez	ils/elles vendent
to answer	répondre	je réponds	tu réponds	il/elle/on répond	nous répondons	vous répondez	ils/elles répondent
to learn	apprendre	j'apprends	tu apprends	il/elle/on apprend	nous apprenons	vous apprenez	ils/elles apprennent
to understand	comprendre	je comprends	tu comprends	il/elle/on comprend	nous comprenons	vous comprenez	ils/elles comprennent
to sell	vendre	je vends	tu vends	il/elle/on vend	nous vendons	vous vendez	ils/elles vendent
to answer	répondre	je réponds	tu réponds	il/elle/on répond	nous répondons	vous répondez	ils/elles répondent
to learn	apprendre	j'apprends	tu apprends	il/elle/on apprend	nous apprenons	vous apprenez	ils/elles apprennent
to understand	comprendre	je comprends	tu comprends	il/elle/on comprend	nous comprenons	vous comprenez	ils/elles comprennent

After present tense, one of the most important tenses to learn in French is "passé compose," or simple past tense. Let's go!

Conjugation to "Passé Composé"

In French, the passé composé is a verb tense used to describe completed actions in the past. It is a compound tense, which means it is formed using two parts: the auxiliary verb (either "avoir" or "être") and the past participle of the main verb. The auxiliary verb is conjugated in the present tense, while the past participle remains unchanged.

For example, in the sentence "J'ai mangé une pomme" (I ate an apple), "ai" is the conjugated form of "avoir" and "mangé" is the past participle of "manger."

The passé composé is commonly used in spoken and written French, especially in casual conversations and narratives. It is often used to describe a single completed action in the past, instead of ongoing or repeated actions.

English	French Infinitive	Past Participle	Avoir Conjugation	Être Conjugation
to have	avoir	eu	j'ai eu	-
to be	être	été	-	j'ai été
to do	faire	fait	j'ai fait	-
to go	aller	allé	je suis allé	-
to see	voir	vu	j'ai vu	-
to take	prendre	pris	j'ai pris	-
to say	dire	dit	j'ai dit	-
to come	venir	venu	je suis venu	-
to know	savoir	su	j'ai su	-
to give	donner	donné	j'ai donné	-

In the Avoir Conjugation column, the subject pronoun is followed by the conjugated form of the verb "avoir" in present tense, and then the past participle of the main verb. For example, "j'ai eu" for "I have had."

In the Être Conjugation column, the subject pronoun is followed by the conjugated form of the verb "être" in present tense, and then the past participle of the main verb. For example, "je suis allé" for "I have gone."

Note that some verbs in French use "avoir" as the helping verb in passé composé, while others use "être." Verbs that use "être" often indicate a change in location or a change in state of being, such as "aller" (to go) or "devenir" (to become).

Now that you have been introduced to passé composé, let's learn about another beloved French tense: Imparfait.

Conjugation to "Imparfait"

In French, "imparfait" or the imperfect tense is a past tense used to describe ongoing or repeated actions in the past. It can be translated to English as "was doing," "used to do," or "would do." The imparfait tense is formed by taking the stem of the infinitive of a verb, and adding a specific set of endings depending on the verb group (-ais, -ais, -ait for verbs ending in -er, -issais, -issais, -issait for for those ending in -ir, and -

ais, -ais, -ait for those ending in -re). For irregular verbs, the stem may also change in the "imparfait" tense.

Imparfait tense			
Pronoun	**-er verb endings**	**-ir verb endings**	**-re verb endings**
je	-ais	-issais	-ais
tu	-ais	-issais	-ais
il/elle	-ait	-issait	-ait
nous	-ions	-issions	-ions
vous	-iez	-issiez	-iez
ils/elles	-aient	-issaient	-aient

English	French infinitive	Je (I)	Tu (singular you)	Il/Elle/On (he/she/one)	Nous (we)	Vous (plural you)	Ils/Elles (they)
to love	aimer	j'aimais	tu aimais	il/elle/on aimait	nous aimions	vous aimiez	ils/elles aimaient
to finish	finir	je finissais	tu finissais	il/elle/on finissait	nous finissions	vous finissiez	ils/elles finissaient
to choose	choisir	je choisissais	tu choisissais	il/elle/on choisissait	nous choisissions	vous choisissiez	ils/elles choisissaient
to punish	punir	je punissais	tu punissais	il/elle/on punissait	nous punissions	vous punissiez	ils/elles punissaient

to succeed	réussir	je réussissais	tu réussissais	il/elle/on réussissait	nous réussissions	vous réussissiez	ils/elles réussissaient
to open	ouvrir	j'ouvrais	tu ouvrais	il/elle/on ouvrait	nous ouvrions	vous ouvriez	ils/elles ouvraient
to suffer	souffrir	je souffrais	tu souffrais	il/elle/on souffrait	nous souffrions	vous souffriez	ils/elles souffraient
to finish	finir	je finissais	tu finissais	il/elle/on finissait	nous finissions	vous finissiez	ils/elles finissaient
to choose	choisir	je choisissais	tu choisissais	il/elle/on choisissait	nous choisissions	vous choisissiez	ils/elles choisissaient
to share	partager	je partageais	tu partageais	il/elle/on partageait	nous partagions	vous partagiez	ils/elles partageaient
to live	vivre	je vivais	tu vivais	il/elle/on vivait	nous vivions	vous viviez	ils/elles vivaient
to sleep	dormir	je dormais	tu dormais	il/elle/on dormait	nous dormions	vous dormiez	ils/elles dormaient
to believe	croire	je croyais	tu croyais	il/elle/on croyait	nous croyions	vous croyiez	ils/elles croyaient
to write	écrire	j'écrivais	tu écrivais	il/elle/on écrivait	nous écrivions	vous écriviez	ils/elles écrivaient
to take	prendre	je prenais	tu prenais	il/elle/on prenait	nous prenions	vous preniez	ils/elles prenaient
to come	venir	je venais	tu venais	il/elle/on venait	nous venions	vous veniez	ils/elles venaient

Chapter 5

Studying or Working in France

If you have the opportunity, studying or working in a French-speaking region will provide you with a unique immersion experience in the French language. This type of experience will lead to faster and more effective learning. This chapter focuses on helping you master the French terminology related to studying and working in such regions.

Let's Learn Some School Vocabulary:

English	French	Pronunciation
student	étudiant(e)	eyt-yoo-dee-ahn(t) / eyt-yoo-dee-ahnt
teacher	professeur(e)	proh-fuh-sir / proh-fuh-sir-ess
class	cours	koors
lesson	leçon	luh-sohn

homework	devoirs	duh-vwar
exam	examen	egz-ah-mahn
test	contrôle	kohn-trohl
grade	note	noht
report card	bulletin scolaire	boo-leh-tahn skoh-lair
backpack	sac à dos	sak ah doh
pen	stylo	stee-loh
pencil	crayon	krah-yohn
notebook	cahier	kah-yay
desk	bureau	byoor-oh
chalkboard	tableau noir	tah-bloh nwahr
eraser	gomme	gom
marker	marqueur	mark-ur
scissors	ciseaux	see-zoh
ruler	règle	rehgl
calculator	calculatrice	kahl-kyuh-lah-treece

As technology improves, it has become more and more integral to our daily lives, making it nearly impossible to avoid using a computer if one chooses to do so. Therefore, let's learn some computer terms.

Computer Terms:

English	French	Pronunciation
computer	ordinateur	ohr-dee-nuh-tuhr
keyboard	clavier	kla-vee-ay
mouse	souris	soo-ree
screen	écran	ay-krahn
printer	imprimante	ahm-pree-mahnt
USB	USB	oo-ess-bee
hard drive	disque dur	deesk durr
software	logiciel	loh-juh-see-ell
hardware	matériel	mah-teh-ree-ell
Internet	Internet	an-tair-nay
email	courriel / email	coor-ree-el / ee-mayl
website	site web	seet wehb
browser	navigateur	nah-vee-gah-tuhr
download	téléchargement	tay-lay-shahrzh-mahnt
upload	téléversement	tay-lay-vehrsmahnt

password	mot de passe	moh duh pahs
username	nom d'utilisateur	nohm dew-tee-lee-za-tehr
wifi	wifi	wee-fee
firewall	pare-feu	pahr-fu

The subsequent lists of vocabulary present several French words frequently used to describe different aspects of the professional world. To facilitate memorization, the categories are divided into verbs and adjectives.

Work Vocabulary

English	French	Pronunciation
job	emploi	ahm-ploah
work	travail	trah-vahy
office	bureau	boor-doh
meeting	réunion	ray-yoon
presentation	présentation	pray-zen-tah-see-yon
project	projet	proh-zhay
deadline	date limite	daht lee-mee-tuh
schedule	horaire	oh-rehr
task	tâche	tahsh

duty	devoir	duh-vwahr
responsibility	responsabilité	reh-spohn-sah-bee-li-tay
skill	compétence	kohm-pay-tahns
experience	expérience	eks-pee-ree-ahns
resume or CV(curriculum vitae)	CV (curriculum vitae)	say-vay
interview	entretien	ahn-truh-tee-yen
salary	salaire	sah-lehr
raise	augmentation	oh-gmohn-tah-see-yon
promotion	promotion	proh-moh-see-yon
contract	contrat	kohn-trah
boss	patron / chef / directeur	pah-trohn / shef / dee-rehk-tuhr
colleague	dollègue	koh-lehg
employee	employé	ahm-ploh-yay
manager	gérant / directeur	zhay-rahnt / dee-rehk-tuhr
company	entreprise	ahn-truh-preez
business	affaires	ah-fehr

Chapter 6

Expanding Your French Vocabulary through Familiar Terms

You can improve your French skills by using French terms to refer to familiar things in your life, such as family members, friends, pets, body parts, and clothing, even if your loved ones don't speak French. While your family and friends might not be interested in playing along, this practice can help you rapidly expand your vocabulary.

Family Vocabulary

English	French	Pronunciation
family	famille	fah-mee
mother	mère	mehr
father	père	pehr
parents	parents	pah-ruh

son	fils	feel
daughter	fille	fee
brother	frère	frehr
sister	soeur	suhr
grandmother	grand-mère	grahn mehr
grandfather	grand-père	grahn pehr
grandparents	grands-parents	grahn pah-ruh
aunt	tante	tahnt
uncle	oncle	ohn-kluh
niece	nièce	nyehs
nephew	neveu	nuh-vuh
cousin (male)	cousin	koo-zuhn
cousin (female)	cousine	koo-zeen
spouse	conjoint(e)	kawn-zwahn (femelle/male)
partner	partenaire	pahr-tuh-nehruh
children	enfants	ahn-fahnt
child	enfant	ahn-fahn
in-laws	beaux-parents	boh-pah-ruh
mother-in-law	belle-mère	behl mehr

father-in-law	beau-père	boh pehr
brother-in-law	beau-frère	boh frehr
sister-in-law	belle-soeur	behl suhr

The vocabulary lists below contain special occasions and holidays that are often celebrated with friends and family.

Holidays Vocabulary

English	French	Pronunciation
holiday	congé, vacances	kawn-jay, vah-kawns
vacation	congé, vacances	kawn-jay, vah-kawns
day off	jour de congé	zhoor duh kawn-jay
weekend	fin de semaine	fahn duh semm
public holiday	jour férié	zhoor fay-ree-ay
Christmas	Noël	noh-el
Easter	Pâques	pahk
New Year's Day	le Jour de l'An	luh zhoor duh lah
Valentine's Day	la Saint-Valentin	lah sahn vah-lahn-tan
Mother's Day	la fête des mères	lah fet day mehr
Father's Day	la fête des pères	lah fet day pair

Independence Day	la fête nationale	lah fet nah-see-oh-nahl
Thanksgiving	l'Action de grâce	lack-see-yohn duh grahs
Halloween	Halloween	hah-loh-een
birthday	anniversaire	ah-nee-vair-sair
anniversary	anniversaire	ah-nee-vair-sair
wedding	mariage	mah-ree-ahzh
reception	réception	ray-sep-see-yohn
gift	cadeau	kah-doh
card	carte	kart
decorations	décorations	day-kor-ah-see-yohn

Now you know what to call the family members that you'll be vacationing with, but what about your friends? Let's learn French vocabulary about friends!

Friends Vocabulary

English	French	Pronunciation
friend	ami(e)	ah-mee
best friend	meilleur(e) ami(e)	mayuhr ah-mee
buddy	copain/copine	koh-pahn/koh-peen

pal	pote	poht
mate	pote	poht
colleague	collègue	koh-lehg
acquaintance	connaissance	koh-nuh-ssahns
teammate	coéquipier/coéquipière	koh-ay-kee-pyeh/koh-ay-kee-pyehr
roommate	colocataire	koh-loh-kah-tair
neighbour	voisin(e)	vwah-zahn
classmate	camarade de classe	kah-mah-rahd duh klahss

Pets are often considered family members or friends to many people, which makes them a great subject for learning new words. The following list includes some of the most common household pets.

Pets Vocabulary

English	French	Pronunciation
cat	chat	sha
dog	chien	shee-ehn
fish	poisson	pwah-son
hamster	hamster	ahm-stehr

guinea pig	cochon d'Inde	koh-shon dan-dee
rabbit	lapin	lah-pan
bird	oiseau	wa-zoh
turtle	tortue	tor-tuh

If you move to France for study or work, you may have to go to the doctor at some point. Therefore, it is useful to know the names of body parts.

Body Parts Vocabulary

English	French	Pronunciation
head	tête	tet
face	visage	vee-zaj
eye	œil	oye
ear	oreille	o-ray
nose	nez	nay
mouth	bouche	boosh
tooth	dent	dahnt
tongue	langue	lawn-g
throat	gorge	gawrj
chest	poitrine	pwah-treen

back	dos	doh
arm	bras	brah
hand	main	mahn
finger	doigt	dwah
leg	jambe	zhamb
knee	genou	zheh-noo
foot	pied	pee-ay
toe	orteil	ohr-tay

You're not going to go to work, school or go out with your friends without getting dressed first, right? Let's learn some vocabulary about clothing in French.

Clothing Vocabulary

English	French	Pronunciation
clothing	vêtements	veh-tuh-mahnt
shirt	chemise	shuh-meez
t-shirt	t-shirt	tee-shert
blouse	blouse	blooz
sweater	pull-over	poo-luh-ver
jacket	veste	vest

coat	manteau	mahn-toh
dress	robe	robe
skirt	jupe	zhewp
pants	pantalon	pahn-tuh-lawn
jeans	jean	zhahn
shorts	short	short
sneakers	baskets	bah-sket
shoes	chaussures	shooh-syur
boots	bottes	boht
sandals	sandales	sahn-dahl
hat	chapeau	shuh-poh
gloves	gants	gahnt
socks	chaussettes	choh-sett
underwear	sous-vêtements	soo-veh-tuh-mahn
swimsuit	maillot de bain	my-yoh duh ban

You're a woman? Ok, let's have a little bit more vocabulary for you:

English	French	Pronunciation
blouse	chemisier	shuh-mee-zee-ay
sweater	pull	poohl
cardigan	gilet	zhee-lay
tank top	débardeur	day-bar-duhr
blazer	veste	vest
skorts	jupe-culotte	zhup koo-lot
leggings	leggings	leh-gings
tights	collants	koh-lahn
bra	soutien-gorge	soo-tee-ahn-gorzh
panties	culotte	koo-lot
bathing suit	maillot de bain	my-yoh duh bahN
high heels	talons hauts	tah-loh oh
flats	ballerines	bah-luh-reen
boots	bottes	boht

We didn't forget about men:

English	French	Pronunciation
polo shirt	polo	poh-loh
suit	costume	kohs-toom
sweater	pull	pool
hoodie	sweat à capuche	swet ah kah-pyoozh
belt	ceinture	sehntoor
tie	cravate	krah-vaht

Now let's also learn some clothing accessories:

English	French	Pronunciation
cap	casquette	kahs-ket
sunglasses	lunettes de soleil	loo-net duh soh-lei
watch	montre	mohnt-ruh
cufflinks	boutons de manchette	boo-tawn duh mahn-shet
pocket square	mouchoir de poche	moo-shwahr duh pohsh
scarf	écharpe	ay-sharp
briefcase	serviette	sehr-vyet
backpack	sac à dos	sak ah doh
wallet	portefeuille	pohrt-fuh-yuh

You are going to talk with your colleagues, friends, comrades... you will probably have to learn colors? So here they are!

Colors in French:

English	French	Pronunciation
black	noir	nwahr
white	blanc	blahn
gray	gris	Gree
brown	marron	mah-rohn
red	rouge	roozh
orange	orange	oh-RAHNSH
yellow	jaune	zhohn
green	Vert	vehrt
blue	bleu	Bluh
purple	violet	vee-oh-LEH
pink	rose	Rohz
gold	or	Or
silver	argent	ahr-zhahnt
bronze	bronze	brohnz
beige	beige	behzh

navy blue	bleu marine	bluh mah-REEN
light blue	bleu clair	bluh klahr
dark blue	bleu foncé	bluh fohn-SAY
pastel	pastel	pah-stell

Chapter 7

Daily Routine and
Home Vocabulary in French

By coming to work or study in France, you will have to find a place to live and adapt to your new daily life. In this chapter, you will find a range of French vocabulary related to your daily routine and your home. A helpful technique to remember these words is to picture each room and the items within it, and then use the corresponding French words to describe them. You could even try walking around the room and naming things as you touch them to reinforce your learning.

This vocabulary list contains French terms for daily activities. It's categorized into morning, afternoon, and evening routines for your convenience.

Vocabulary about Morning Routines

English	French	Pronunciation
wake up	se réveiller	suh ray-vay-yay
get out of bed	sortir du lit	sor-teer doo lee
brush your teeth	se brosser les dents	suh broh-say lay dahnt
take a shower	prendre une douche	prahn-druhn dewsh
wash your face	se laver le visage	suh lah-vay luh vee-sahzh
comb your hair	se peigner les cheveux	suh peh-nyay lay shevuh
get dressed	s'habiller	sab-ee-yay
have breakfast	prendre le petit-déjeuner	prahn-druh luh puh-tee-day-zhuh-nay
drink coffee	boire du café	bwah-r duh kah-fay
check your email	vérifier ses e-mails	vay-ree-fyay sayz ee-mayl
go to work	aller au travail	ah-lay oh trah-vahy
arrive at work	arriver au travail	ah-ree-vay oh trah-vahy
start working	commencer à travailler	koh-mahn-say ah trah-vah-yay

Vocabulary about Afternoon Routines

English	French	Pronunciation
lunch	déjeuner	day-zheuh-nay
nap	sieste	see-est
coffee	café	kah-fay
tea	thé	tay
snack	collation	koh-lah-syohn
work	travail	trah-vahy
meeting	réunion	reuh-nyohn
phone call	appel téléphonique	ah-pel tay-lay-foh-neek
errands	courses	koor-sus
exercise	exercice	eg-zehr-sees
hobbies	loisirs	lwah-zeer

Vocabulary about Evening Routines

English	French	Pronunciation
dinner	dîner	dee-nay
dessert	dessert	deh-sehr
wash the dishes	laver la vaisselle	lah-vay lah vay-sell

clean up	ranger	rahn-jay
watch TV	regarder la télévision	ruh-gahr-day lah tay-lay-vee-zee-yon
read a book	lire un livre	leer uh(n) lee-vruh
take a bath	prendre un bain	prahn-druh uh(n) behn
take a shower	prendre une douche	prahn-druh yoon doosh
brush teeth	se brosser les dents	suh bross-ay lay dahn
go to bed	aller se coucher	ah-lay suh coo-shay
sleep	dormir	dohr-meer
dream	rêver	reh-vay
goodnight	bonne nuit	bawn nwee

You can expand your vocabulary by taking a tour of your home and identifying the following items.

Vocabulary about Home Furniture

English	French	Pronunciation
armchair	fauteuil	foh-tuh-yuh
bed	lit	lee
bedside table	table de nuit	tahbl duh nwee

bench	banc	bahn
bookcase	bibliothèque	bee-blee-oh-tek
carpet	tapis	tah-pee
fan	ventilateur	vahn-tee-luh-tur
chair	chaise	Shez
chandelier	lustre	loo-struh
chest of drawers	commode	kuh-mohd
coffee table	table basse	tahbl bass
curtains	rideaux	ree-doh
desk	bureau	boor-oh
dining table	table à manger	tahbl ah mahn-jay
dressing table	coiffeuse	kwah-fuz
end table	table d'appoint	tahbl dah-pwahn
fireplace	cheminée	shuh-mee-neh
floor lamp	lampadaire	lahm-puh-dehr
footstool	repose-pieds	ruh-pohz-pee-ay
futon	futon	foo-tawn
hanger	cintre	Santr
heater	radiateur	rah-dee-uh-tur

lamp	lampe	lahm-puh
lazy boy	fauteuil inclinable	foh-tuh-yuh an-klee-nahbl
mirror	miroir	mee-rwahr
nightstand	table de nuit	tahbl duh nwee
ottoman	ottomane	oh-tuh-mahn
painting	tableau	tah-bloh
picture frame	cadre	kah-druh
pillow	oreiller	oh-ray-yay
recliner	fauteuil inclinable	foh-tuh-yuh an-klee-nahbl
rug	tapis	tah-pee
screen	paravent	pah-rah-vahn
shelving unit	étagère	ay-tah-zhehr
shoe rack	porte-chaussures	port shoh-syur
side table	table d'appoint	tahbl dah-pwahn
sofa	canapé	kah-nah-pay
stool	tabouret	tah-boor-ay
table lamp	lampe de table	lahm-puh duh tahbl
television	télévision	tay-lay-vee-zee-ohn

throw pillow	coussin décoratif	koo-sahn day-koh-rah-tif
towel rack	porte-serviette	port sehr-vyett
TV stand	meuble télé	muh-bl tay-lay
vase	Vase	Vahz
wall clock	horloge murale	ohr-lozh moo-rahl
wardrobe	armoire	ar-mwahr
window	fenêtre	fuh-neh-truh
window blinds	stores	Stohr

Now that you can identify the items in your home, what about the rooms in your house?

Vocabulary about Rooms

English	French	Pronunciation
living room	le salon	luh sah-lon
dining room	la salle à manger	lah sahl ah mahn-zhay
kitchen	la cuisine	lah kwee-zeen
bedroom	la chambre	lah shahm-bruh
bathroom	la salle de bain	lah sahl duh ban
toilet	les toilettes	lay twah-let

attic	le grenier	luh gruh-nyay
basement	le sous-sol	luh soo-sohl
office/study	le bureau	luh byur-oh
library	la bibliothèque	lah bee-blee-oh-teck
playroom	la salle de jeux	lah sahl duh zhuh
guest room	la chambre d'amis	lah shahm-bruh dah-mee
laundry room	la buanderie	lah boh-ahn-duh-ree
garage	le garage	luh gah-rahj
garden	le jardin	luh zhar-dahn
terrace/balcony	la terrasse/le balcon	lah teh-rahs/luh bahl-kohn
porch	le porche	luh porch

Living in a house might be great, however in France, especially big cities like Paris, chances are you'll live in an apartment instead. Let's discover useful vocabulary if you are preparing to live in an apartment.

Vocabulary about Apartments

English	French	Pronunciation
apartment	appartement	ah-par-tuh-mahn

building	immeuble	eem-uh-bluh
elevator	ascenseur	ah-sawn-sir
stairs	escalier	es-kah-lee-ay
door	porte	port
window	fenêtre	fuh-net-ruh
balcony	balcon	bal-kohn
kitchen	cuisine	kwee-zeen
bathroom	salle de bains	sahl duh ban
toilet	toilette	twa-let
shower	douche	doosh
sink	lavabo	lah-vah-bo
mirror	miroir	mee-rwahr
key	clé	klay
lease	bail	bahy
rent	loyer	loy-ey
landlord	propriétaire	pro-pree-uh-tair
tenant	locataire	loh-kuh-tair
utilities	services publics	sehr-vees poo-bleek
electricity	électricité	ay-lek-tree-see-tay

gas	gaz	gahz
water	eau	oh
Internet	Internet	een-tuhr-net
cable	câble	kah-bl

I don't know about you, but as far as I'm concerned, my favorite room is the kitchen (yes, I love to eat!). And if you come to live in France, you will also need to eat.

Kitchen and Market Items:

English	French	Pronunciation
apron	tablier	tah-blee-ay
baking tray	plaque à pâtisserie	plak ah pah-tee-suh-ree
blender	mixeur	mee-zeur
bowl	bol	bohl
can opener	ouvre-boîte	oovr bwat
coffee maker	cafetière	kaf-uh-tyehr
colander	passoire	pah-swahr
cooking pot	casserole	kah-suh-rohl
cutting board	planche à découper	plahnsh ah day-koo-pay

dish	plat	plah
dish towel	torchon	tor-shawn
fork	fourchette	foohr-shet
freezer	congélateur	kohn-zheh-luh-tuhr
frying pan	poêle	pohl
glass	verre	vehr
grater	râpe	rahp
kitchen scale	balance de cuisine	bah-lahns duh kwee-zeen
knife	couteau	koo-toh
measuring cup	tasse à mesurer	tahs ah meh-zuh-ray
microwave	micro-ondes	mee-kroh ohnd
mixing bowl	saladier	sah-lah-dyehr
oven	four	foor
pan	poêle	pohl
pot	casserole	kah-suh-rohl
refrigerator	réfrigérateur	reh-free-juh-rah-tuhr
saucepan	casserole	kah-suh-rohl
spoon	cuillère	kwee-yehr

stove	cuisinière	kwee-zi-nyehr
toaster	grille-pain	greel-pahn
whisk	fouet	foo-ay

Great, now you know the items you can have in your kitchen to prepare food. But you will also need food. The vocabulary lists below consist of various French words for grocery and food items. They are categorized to aid you in memorization.

Vegetables in French:

English	French	Pronunciation
asparagus	asperge(s)	ah-spairzh
broccoli	brocoli	broh-koh-lee
carrot	carotte	kuh-rott
cauliflower	chou-fleur	shoo-fluhr
corn	maïs	meh-ees
cucumber	concombre	kon-kohm-bruh
eggplant	aubergine	oh-behr-jeen
garlic	ail	ah-eel
green beans	haricots verts	ah-ree-koh vair
lettuce	laitue	leh-tew

onion	oignon	ohn-yohn
peas	petits pois	peh-tee pwah
pepper	poivron	pwah-vrohn
potato	pomme de terre	pohm duh tehr
spinach	épinards	ay-pee-nahr
squash	courge	koorg
tomato	tomate	toh-maht
zucchini	courgette(s)	koor-zheht

Fruits in French:

English	French	Pronunciation
apple	pomme	pohm
apricot	abricot	ah-bree-koh
avocado	avocat	ah-voh-kah
banana	banane	bah-nahn
blackberry	mûre	mewr
blueberry	myrtille	meer-teel
cherry	cerise	seh-reez
coconut	noix de coco	nwah deh koh-koh
cranberry	canneberge	kahn-behrzh

fig	figue	feeg
grape	raisin	reh-zahn
grapefruit	pamplemousse	pahm-pleh-moos
lemon	citron	see-trohn
lime	citron vert	see-trohn vehrt
mango	mangue	mahn-guh
orange	orange	oh-rahnj
peach	pêche	pesh
pear	poire	pwahr
pineapple	ananas	ah-nah-nahs
plum	prune	proon
raspberry	framboise	frahm-bwahz
strawberry	fraise	frehz
watermelon	pastèque	pah-stek

Food Staples in French

English	French	Pronunciation
bread	pain	pahn
milk	lait	lay
eggs	œufs	uhf

cheese	fromage	froh-mahzh
rice	riz	reez
pasta	pâtes	paht
sugar	sucre	soo-kruh
salt	sel	sell
oil	huile	weel
butter	beurre	buhr

Meat, Poultry, Seafood, and Eggs in French

English	French	Pronunciation
beef	bœuf	buhf
chicken	poulet	poo-lay
pork	porc	pohrk
lamb	agneau	ahn-yoh
veal	veau	voh
ham	jambon	zham-bohn
bacon	bacon	bah-kon
sausage	saucisse	soh-sees
hotdog	chien chaud	shee-ehn shoh
salami	salami	sah-lah-mee
shrimp	crevette	kreh-vet

crab	crabe	krahb
lobster	homard	oh-mahr
clam	palourde	pah-loord
oyster	huître	wee-truh
mussel	moule	mool
scallop	coquille Saint-Jacques	koh-keel sahn zhahk
squid	calmar	kahl-mahr
octopus	pieuvre	pee-evr
cod	morue	moh-ruh
trout	truite	trweet
salmon	saumon	soh-mohn
tuna	thon	tohn
crabmeat	chair de crabe	shair duh krahb
lobster meat	chair de homard	shair duh oh-mahr
ground beef	viande hachée	vyahnd ah-shay
steak	steak	stayk
roast beef	rôti de boeuf	roh-tee duh buhf
lamb chops	côtelettes d'agneau	koht-luht duh ahn-yoh
chicken breast	blanc de poulet	blahn duh poo-lay

Et bon appétit!

Chapter 8

Extensive Dictionary

Now that you are prepared to come to France whether for holidays, to work or to study, we offer you an extensive dictionary that will allow you to have even more vocabulary.

Practice Your Vocabulary

Basic vocabulary - This includes essential words and phrases for greeting people, introducing yourself, expressing emotions, and making basic requests :

English	French	Pronunciation
Hello	Bonjour	bohn-zhoor
Goodbye	Au revoir	oh ruh-vwahr
Please	S'il vous plaît	seel voo pleh
Thank you	Merci	mehr-see

Excuse me	Excusez-moi	eks-kyoo-zay mwah
Yes	Oui	wee
No	Non	nohn
I	Je	zhuh
You	Vous/Tu	voo/too
He	Il	eel
She	Elle	ell
We	Nous	noo
They	Ils/Elles	eel/el
What?	Quoi?	kwah
Who?	Qui?	kee
When?	Quand?	kahn
Where?	Où?	oo
Why?	Pourquoi?	poor-kwah
How?	Comment?	koh-mahn
My name is...	Je m'appelle...	zhuh mah-pehl
Nice to meet you	Enchanté(e)	ahn-shahn-tey/tey
Good morning	Bonjour (le matin)	bohn-zhoor (luh ma-tahn)

Good afternoon	Bon après-midi	bohn ah-preh-mee-dee
Good evening	Bonsoir	bohn-swahr
Good night	Bonne nuit	bohn nwee
See you later	À plus tard	ah ploos tar
See you soon	À bientôt	ah byen-toh
Good luck	Bonne chance	bohn shahns
Cheers!	Santé!	sahn-tay
Congratulations	Félicitations	fay-lee-see-tah-syoh
Happy birthday	Joyeux anniversaire	zhwa-yuh ah-nee-vair-sair
I'm sorry	Je suis désolé(e)	zhuh swee day-zoh-lay
Help!	Au secours!	oh seh-coor!
Good	Bon(ne)	bohn/bohn
Bad	Mauvais(e)	moh-vay/moh-vayz
Big	Grand(e)	grahnd/grahnd
Small	Petit(e)	puh-tee/puh-tee
Hot	Chaud(e)	shoh/shohd
Cold	Froid(e)	fwah/fwahd
Beautiful	Beau/belle	boh/bell

Ugly	Laid(e)	lay/led
Cheap	Bon marché	bohn mar-shay
Expensive	Cher/Chère	shair/shair
Easy	Facile	fah-seel
Difficult	Difficile	dee-fee-seel
Goodbye (informal)	Salut	sah-lood
See you tomorrow	À demain	ah duh-mehn
See you soon	À tout à l'heure	ah too-tah-luhr
Excuse me (getting past someone)	Pardon	pahr-dohn
Excuse me (to get someone's attention)	Excusez-moi	eks-kyoo-zay mwah

Numbers - Learning the French numbers is crucial for everyday communication, such as telling the time, giving your phone number, or ordering at a restaurant:

English	French	Pronunciation
zero	zéro	zeh-roh
one	un/une	uh/oon
two	deux	duh
three	trois	twah

four	quatre	kah-truh
five	cinq	sank
six	six	sees
seven	sept	set
eight	huit	wheat
nine	neuf	nurf
ten	dix	dees
eleven	onze	ohnz
twelve	douze	dooz
thirteen	treize	trehz
fourteen	quatorze	kah-torz
fifteen	quinze	kanz
sixteen	seize	sehz
seventeen	dix-sept	dees-set
eighteen	dix-huit	dees-wheat
nineteen	dix-neuf	dees-nurf
twenty	vingt	vahn
twenty-one	vingt et un	vahn ay uh
twenty-two	vingt-deux	vahn-duh

English	French	Pronunciation
thirty	trente	trahnt
forty	quarante	kah-rahnt
fifty	cinquante	sa(n)-kahnt
sixty	soixante	swah-sahnt
seventy	soixante-dix	swah-sahnt-dees
eighty	quatre-vingts	kah-truh-va(n)
ninety	quatre-vingt-dix	dah-truh-va(n)-dees
one hundred	cent	sah(n)
one thousand	mille	meel
one million	un million	uh(n) mee-lee-yohn

Colors - Knowing the colors in French is important for describing objects and places, and for fashion and design:

English	French	Pronunciation
black	noir	nwahr
white	blanc	blahn
gray	gris	Gree
brown	marron	mah-rohn
red	rouge	roozh
orange	orange	oh-RAHNSH
yellow	jaune	zhohn

green	Vert	vehrt
blue	bleu	Bluh
purple	violet	vee-oh-LEH
pink	rose	Rohz
gold	or	Or
silver	argent	ahr-zhahnt
bronze	bronze	brohnz
beige	beige	behzh
navy blue	bleu marine	bluh mah-REEN
light blue	bleu clair	bluh klahr
dark blue	bleu foncé	bluh fohn-SAY
pastel	pastel	pah-stell

Days of the week, months, and seasons - These words are used in many different contexts, from making appointments to planning vacations:

Days of the week:

English	French	Pronunciation
Monday	lundi	luhn-dee
Tuesday	mardi	mar-dee
Wednesday	mercredi	mehr-kruh-dee
Thursday	jeudi	juh-dee

Friday	vendredi	vahn-druh-dee
Saturday	samedi	sahm-dee
Sunday	dimanche	dee-mahnsh

Months:

English	French	Pronunciation
January	janvier	zhahn-vee-yay
February	février	fay-vree-yay
March	mars	marss
April	avril	ah-vreel
May	mai	mey
June	juin	zhwan
July	juillet	zhwee-yay
August	août	oot
September	septembre	set-tuhm-bruh
October	octobre	ok-tuh-bruh
November	novembre	noh-vuhm-bruh
December	décembre	day-sahm-bruh

Seasons:

English	French	Pronunciation
spring	le printemps	luh prahn-tahm
summer	l'été	lay-tay
fall / autumn	l'automne	loh-tohm
winter	l'hiver	lee-vair

Family and relationships - Vocabulary related to family members, personal relationships, and social interactions is essential for building connections with French speakers:

English	French	Pronunciation
family	la famille	lah fah-mee
mother	la mère	lah mehr
father	le père	luh pehr
son	le fils	luh feels
daughter	la fille	lah feel
brother	le frère	luh frehr
sister	la sœur	lah suhr
grandmother	la grand-mère	lah grahN-mehr
grandfather	le grand-père	luh grahN-pehr
grandson	le petit-fils	luh peh-tee feelss

granddaughter	la petite-fille	lah peh-tee feel
uncle	l'oncle	lohN-kluh
aunt	la tante	lah tahNt
niece	la niece	lah nyess
nephew	le neveu	luh neh-vuh
cousin (male)	le cousin	luh koo-zaN
cousin (female)	la cousine	lah koo-zeen
godfather	le parrain	luh pah-raN
godmother	la marraine	lah mah-rehn
friend	l'ami (male)/l'amie (female)	lah-mee/lah-mee-uh
boyfriend	le petit ami	luh peh-tee ah-mee
girlfriend	la petite amie	lah peh-tee ah-mee
partner	le partenaire/ la partenaire	luh pahr-tuh-nair/ lah pahr-tuh-nair
fiancé	le fiancé	luh fee-ahn-say
fiancée	la fiancée	lah fee-ahn-say
spouse	le conjoint/ la conjointe	luh kohN-zhwa/ lah kohN-zhwaNt
husband	le mari	luh mah-ree
wife	la femme	lah fehm
divorce	le divorce	luh dee-vohrs
separation	la séparation	lah say-pah-ra-syohN
single	célibataire	say-lee-bah-tair

English	French	Pronunciation
married	marié(e)	mah-ree-eh
children	les enfants	lay-zahN-fahN
son-in-law	le gendre	luh zhahNdruh
daughter-in-law	la belle-fille	lah behl-feel
mother-in-law	la belle-mère	lah behl-mehr
father-in-law	le beau-père	luh boh-pehr
brother-in-law	le beau-frère	luh boh-frehR
sister-in-law	la belle-sœur	lah behl-suhr

Food and drink - French cuisine is renowned worldwide, and knowing the vocabulary for food and drink is essential for ordering at restaurants or shopping at markets:

English	French	Pronunciation
appetizer	l'entrée	lahn-tray
main course	le plat principal	luh plah pruhn-seepal
dessert	le dessert	luh deh-sehr
salad	la salade	lah sah-lahd
soup	la soupe	lah soo-puh
sandwich	le sandwich	luh sahn-dweesh
bread	le pain	luh pan
butter	le beurre	luh buhr

cheese	le fromage	luh fro-mahj
meat	la viande	lah vee-ahnd
beef	le boeuf	luh buhf
pork	le porc	luh pohrk
chicken	le poulet	luh poo-lay
fish	le poisson	luh pwah-sohn
seafood	les fruits de mer	lay frwee duh mehr
shrimp	la crevette	lah kreh-vet
lobster	le homard	luh oh-mar
crab	le crabe	luh krahb
oyster	l'huître	lee-tre
mussel	la moule	lah mool
clam	la palourde	lah pah-loord
vegetable	le légume	luh lay-goom
potato	la pomme de terre	lah pohm duh tair
carrot	la carotte	lah kuh-rot
broccoli	le brocoli	luh broh-koh-lee
tomato	la tomate	lah toh-maht
onion	l'oignon	lohn-yohn

garlic	l'ail	
fruit	le fruit	
apple	la pomme	
banana	la banane	ɔan-nahn
orange	l'orange	lor-ahnj
peach	la pêche	lah pesh
grape	le raisin	luh reh-zan
cherry	la cerise	lah seh-reez
strawberry	la fraise	lah frehz
beverage	la boisson	lah bwah-sohn
water	l'eau	loh
soda	le soda	luh soh-dah
coffee	le café	luh kah-fay
tea	le thé	luh tay
wine	le vin	luh van
beer	la bière	lah byehr
champagne	le champagne	luh sham-pahn
cocktail	le cocktail	luh kohk-tayl

sportation - Vocabulary related to transportation is essential for navigating cities and getting around, whether by car, train, or bus:

English Word	French Word	Pronunciation
car	la voiture	lah vwah-tour
bus	le bus	luh boos
train	le train	luh trah-ehn
subway/metro	le metro	luh may-troh
bicycle	le vélo	luh vay-loh
motorcycle	la moto	lah mo-toh
scooter	le scooter	luh skoo-ter
airplane	l'avion	lah-vee-ohn
airport	l'aéroport	lah-ay-roh-por
ticket	le billet	luh bee-yay
one-way ticket	l'aller simple	lah-lay sim-pluh
round-trip ticket	l'aller-retour	lah-lay ruh-toor
platform	le quai	luh kai
station	la gare	lah gahr
stop (on a bus or train)	l'arrêt	lah-ray

traffic jam	les embouteillages	lay-zahm-boo-tay
parking lot	le parking	luh par-king
gas station	la station-service	lah stah-syon-sehr-vees
highway	l'autoroute	loh-toh-root
street	la rue	lah roo
intersection	le carrefour	luh kahr-foo
bridge	le pont	luh pohn
tunnel	le tunnel	luh too-nel
sidewalk	le trottoir	luh troh-twahr
pedestrian	le piéton	luh pee-eh-tohn
lane	la voie	lah vwah
speed limit	la limitation de vitesse	lah lee-mee-tah-syon duh vee-tess
driver's license	le permis de conduire	luh pair-mee duh kohn-dweer
car rental	la location de voiture	lah loh-kah-syon duh vwah-tour

Clothing and fashion - France is a center of fashion, and knowing the vocabulary related to clothing and fashion is important for social and professional contexts:

English	French	Pronunciation
clothing	les vêtements	lay vayt-mahn
shirt	la chemise	lah shuh-meez
t-shirt	le T-shirt	luh tee-shirt
blouse	la blouse	lah blooz
sweater	le pull	luh pool
cardigan	le cardigan	luh kar-dee-gahn
jacket	la veste	lah vest
coat	le manteau	luh mahn-toh
dress	la robe	lah rohb
skirt	la jupe	lah zhup
pants	le pantalon	luh pahn-tuh-lohn
jeans	le jean	luh zhahn
shorts	le short	luh shohrt
underwear	les sous-vêtements	lay soo-vayt-mahn
socks	les chaussettes	lay shoh-set
shoes	les chaussures	lay shohz-yoor
sneakers	les baskets	lay bas-ket
sandals	les sandales	lay san-dahl
boots	les bottes	lay both
high heels	les talons hauts	lay tah-lawn oh
belt	la ceinture	lah sahn-tur
scarf	l'écharpe	lay-sharp

gloves	les gants	lay gahn
hat	le chapeau	luh shuh-poh
sunglasses	les lunettes de soleil	lay loo-net deh soh-leh
jewelry	les bijoux	lay bee-zhoo
watch	la montre	lah mohnt
earrings	les boucles d'oreilles	lay boo-kluh doh-reh-yuh
necklace	le collier	luh koh-lee-ay
bracelet	le bracelet	luh brah-slay
ring	la bague	lah bahg

Work and business - Vocabulary related to work and business is essential for professional contexts, whether you're looking for a job or conducting business in French:

English	French	Pronunciation
job	le travail	luh trah-vah-yuh
career	la carrière	lah kah-ryehr
employment	l'emploi	lahmp-loi
résumé/CV	le curriculum vitae	luh kyoor-ree-kyooluhm vee-tahy
interview	l'entretien d'embauche	lah(n)-truh-tyeh(n) dah(n)-boosh
manager	le/la manager	luh/la(man-ah-jay)
employee	l'employé(e)	lah(n)-ploy-ay

boss	le patron / la patronne	luh pah-trawn / lah pah-trawn
office	le bureau	luh boo-roh
colleague	le/la collègue	luh/la(koh-lehg)
meeting	la reunion	lah(reuh-nyoh(n))
presentation	la presentation	lah(pre-zahn-tahsyoh(n))
conference	la conference	lah(koh(n)-feh-rah(n)s)
business trip	le voyage d'affaires	luh vwah-yahzh dah-fehr
sales	les ventes	lay(vahnt)
marketing	le marketing	luh mahr-kuh-ting
accounting	la comptabilité	lah koh(n)-tah-bee-li-tay
finance	la finance	lah feh-nah(n)s
investment	l'investissement	la(n)vess-tees-mah(n)
stock market	la bourse	lah boors
entrepreneur	l'entrepreneur	lah(n)-truh-pruh-nuhr
start-up	la start-up	lah stahrt-up
salary	le salaire	luh sah-lehr
raise	l'augmentation	loh(g-mahn-tah-syoh(n))
promotion	la promotion	lah proh-moh-syoh(n)

English	French	Pronunciation
benefits	les avantages	lay(zah-vah(n)-tahzh)
retirement	la retraite	lah ruh-treht
pension	la pension	lah pah(n)-syoh(n)
union	le syndicat	luh sa(n)-dee-kah
contract	le contrat	luh koh(n)-trah
agreement	l'accord	lah-kohr
deadline	la date limite	lah daht lee-meet
productivity	la productivité	lah proh-dewk-tee-vee-tay
efficiency	l'efficacité	leff-ee-kah-say-tee

Common verbs and grammar - A basic knowledge of French verbs and grammar is essential for constructing sentences and communicating effectively:

English	French	Pronunciation
to be	être	et-ruh
to have	avoir	ah-vwahr
to do/make	faire	fehr
to say	dire	deer
to go	aller	ah-lay
to come	venir	vuh-neer
to see	voir	vwar
to want	vouloir	voo-lwahr

to know	savoir	sa-vwahr
to think	penser	pahn-say
to speak	parler	pahr-lay
to understand	comprendre	kohm-prahn-druh
to give	donner	doh-nay
to like	aimer	em-ay
to love	aimer beaucoup	em-ay boo-koo
to hate	détester	day-teh-stay
to need	avoir besoin de	ah-vwahr buh-zwahn duh
to try	essayer	ess-ay-ay
to work	travailler	trah-vah-yay
to study	étudier	ay-tew-dyay
to write	écrire	ay-kreer
to read	lire	leer
to listen	écouter	ay-koo-tay
to watch	regarder	ruh-gahr-day
to eat	manger	mahn-jay
to drink	boire	bwahr
to cook	cuisiner	kwee-zee-nay
to sleep	dormir	dohr-meer
to wake up	se réveiller	suh reh-vay-yay
to get up	se lever	suh luh-vay

to take	prendre	prahn-druh
to give back	rendre	rahn-druh
to buy	acheter	ah-shuh-tay
to sell	vendre	vahn-druh
to pay	payer	pay-yay
to open	ouvrir	oo-vree
to close	fermer	fehr-may
to start/begin	commencer	koh-mahn-say
to finish/end	finir	fee-neer
to arrive	arriver	ah-ree-vay
to leave	partir	pahr-teer
to stay	rester	reh-stay
to return	retourner	ruh-toor-nay
to miss	manquer	mahn-kay
to forget	oublier	oo-blee-yay
to remember	se souvenir de	suh soo-vehn-eer duh
to use	utiliser	oo-tee-lee-zay
to change	changer	shahn-jay
to help	aider	ay-day
to hope	espérer	ess-pay-ray
to wait	attendre	ah-tahn-druh
to meet	rencontrer	rahn-kohn-tray

to call	appeler	ah-peh-lay
to send	envoyer	ahn-vwah-yay
to receive	recevoir	ruh-suh-vwahr
to ask	demander	dahn-mahn-day
to answer	répondre	reh-pohndruh

We hope you enjoyed learning French with us! Feel free to review the above chapters and use our dictionary whenever you need it. A bientôt!

LEAVE A REVIEW

If you liked this Ebook, I would be extremely happy and grateful if you left a comment. Please take a few minutes to leave a comment by scanning this QR code, this will allow me to continue to offer you quality educational content.

Printed in Great Britain
by Amazon

24422617R00065